Would Your Dog Rather Game Book For Kids and Dog Lovers of All Ages

A Collection of Silly Scenarios and Humorous Questions that the Whole Family Will Enjoy

By K. B. Parilli

ISBN-13: 978-1-947238-69-5

DeGrawPublishing@comcast.net
De Graw Publishing
Lady Lake, Florida

Would your dog rather...

Wear a collar  OR **wear a raincoat?**

Walk a mile  OR **sit still for an hour?**

Would your dog rather...

Eat celery
OR
go hungry?

Play dead
OR
run a
marathon?

Would your dog rather...

Eat cabbage
OR
sit in the rain?

Go on a trip
OR
eat pizza?

Would your dog rather...

Steal a bite of your food

OR

eat a whole box of bones?

Be carried everywhere

OR

go on a long hike?

Would your dog rather...

Sleep on the sofa

OR

beg you food?

Go camping

OR

lazy around the pool?

Would your dog rather...

Hang out with you **OR** play with a stranger?

Eat coconut cream pie **OR** a slice of steak?

Would your dog rather...

Watch TV all day OR swim in the pool?

Eat mangos OR lasagna?

Would your dog rather...

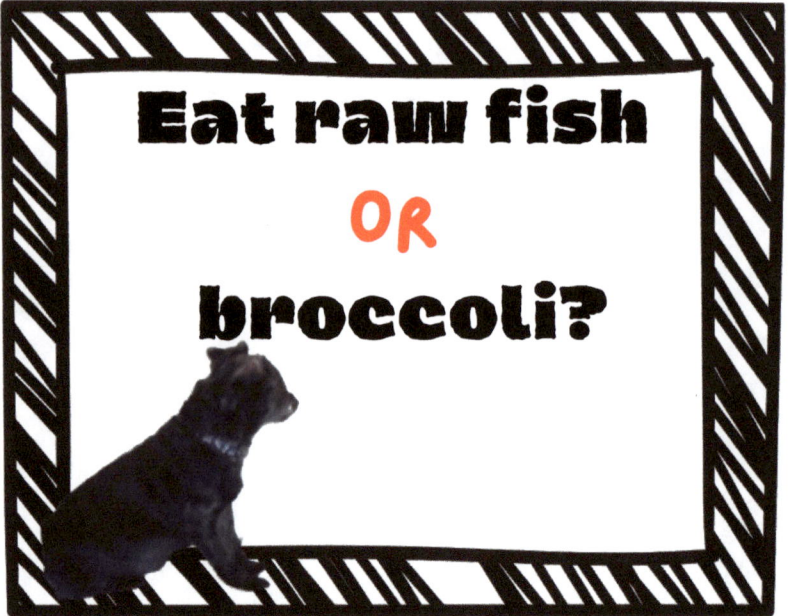

Eat raw fish OR broccoli?

Eat French fries OR ice cream?

Would your dog rather...

Own his own
pet store
OR
a burger shop?

Hire a
chauffer
OR
cook?

Would your dog rather...

Get a massage **OR** win a thousand bones?

Chase his tail **OR** run an obstacle course?

Would your dog rather...

Win a trophy

OR

or have his picture in the papers?

live in a fancy apartment

OR

camp in the woods?

Would your dog rather...

Earn a reward

OR

sneak some food?

Eat a slice of apple

OR

have a timeout?

Would your dog rather...

Eat a sundae **OR** drink a milkshake?

Ride in the front seat **OR** sleep in the back seat?

Would your dog rather...

Win a vacation around the world **OR** win an cookie?

Be covered in mud **OR** enjoy a manicure?

Would your dog rather...

Take a bath
OR
smell like a skunk for a month?

Be best in show
OR
an off-road champ?

Would your dog rather...

Chase a cat

OR

eat lunch?

Learn to surf

OR

channel surf?

Would your dog rather...

Be king of the road

OR

king of the kitchen?

Own a dozen beds

OR

a popcorn maker?

Would your dog rather...

Go the vet
OR
go without
breakfast?

Eat bread and
water
OR
wear a
sweater?

Would your dog rather...

Go fishing
OR
go for a walk
in the park?

Take a ride on
a boat
OR
a
rollercoaster?

Would your dog rather...

Travel the country by train

OR

RV?

Make friends with 20 dogs

OR

the owner of the pizza palace?

Would your dog rather...

Be a contestant on top dog **OR** top chef?

Be silent for a week **OR** skip a meal?

Would your dog rather...

Ride in a
race car
OR
learn to
skydive?

Have a million
subscriber You
Tube Channel
OR
a restaurant?

Would your dog rather...

Vacation at
the beach
OR
the mountains?

Stay in an
airconditioned
hotel
OR
under the stars?

Would your dog rather...

Eat dog food

OR

fruit salad?

Have a bone account

OR

a dog walker?

Would your dog rather...

Swim with seals **OR** explore the outback?

Watch a cooking show **OR** listen to dogs howl?

Would your dog rather...

Spend the day at a waterpark **OR** go for a balloon ride?

Learn to navigate a maze **OR** learn to fetch?

Would your dog rather...

Spend a day
at the groomer
OR
watching
grass grow?

Have his teeth
brushed
OR
get a shot?

Would your dog rather...

Watch lions
OR
monkeys at
the zoo?

Be a
bloodhound
Or
a doggy
Einstein?

Would your dog rather...

Get hugs

OR

kisses?

Foster a flock
of chickens

OR

twin goats?

Would your dog rather...

Spend a night in the desert

OR

kennel?

Be called king of your heart

OR

king of your pocketbook?

Other Activity Books You Might Enjoy

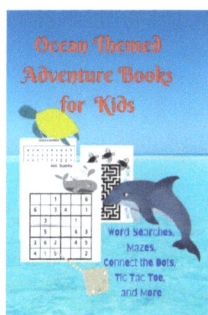

Ocean Themed Adventure Books for Kids
Word Searches, Mazes, Connect the Dots, Tic Tac Toe, and More

Enjoy this fun-packed collection of ocean themed activities. This activity book contains a wonderful assortment of ocean inspired word searches, mazes, word scrambles, sudoku puzzles, find the difference, and more. Bring home the adventure, and flex your mental muscles with this collection of oceans inspired delight.

Simple Kaleidoscope Style Coloring Book for Kids:
Vol1
Silly Shape Fun

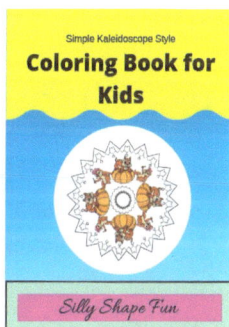

Enjoy the fun and creativity of Silly Shape Fun.

Your child will appreciate

28 whimsical images to color

A comfortable 8.5" by 11" format

Single-sided pages: Reducing the issue with bleed through.

Great for all skill levels: There is no wrong way to color the pictures making it an excellent choice for all skill levels.

Bring home the fun today

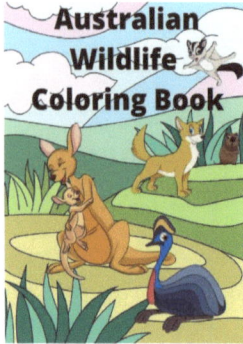

Australian Wildlife Coloring Book
25 Fun and Relaxing Australian Animals Coloring Pages

Take a break from the uncertainty of life and enjoy this relaxing collection of adorable Australian animal life. Let your creative juices flow. Give yourself the gift of some guilt free quiet time that will keep your children entertained while letting their creative juices flow. Or enjoy some parent child time as you talk and color together.

Country Dot to Dot   a Delightful Collection of Animal and Cowboy Dot to Dots Ages 7 and Up

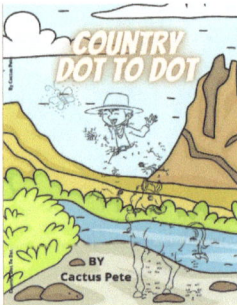

Bring home hours of country themed, dot to dot fun for your kids! This entertaining and brain stimulating dot to dot book features:

118 animal and cowboy dot to dot puzzles

Animals and cowboys ranging from 20 to 100 dots

Helps to build fine motor skills and eye hand coordination skills

Easy to carry 6 in by 9-inch format

Images can be colored once the dots are connected

Makes an excellent gift

Bring home a copy today!

www.ingramcontent.com/pod-product-compliance
Lightning Source LLC
Chambersburg PA
CBHW041807040426

42448CB00005B/299